# The Young Scientist Book of STARS & PLANETS

It takes a well-trained eye to read the sky and a wide range of telescopes and probes to study it in detail. Here are just some of the tools astronomers use to look at the universe.

Orbiting observatories like OAO-3 enable astronomers to photograph the stars without having to peer through Earth's murky atmosphere.

A prism splits light into a rainbow of colour called a spectrum. By studying the spectrum of a star's light, astronomers can find out about its make-up.

The 100 m Effelsburg dish near Bonn in Germany is the biggest rotating radio telescope in the world. Such giant 'telescope ears' let scientists probe deep into the universe.

The 66 cm Washington refractor telescope was built in 1862. Astronomers using it discovered the moons of Mars and the companion star of Sirius.

1

# CREDITS

**Written by**
Christopher Maynard
**Art and editorial direction**
David Jefferis
**Design assistant**
Iain Ashman

**Scientific advisors**
Adrian Berry, FRAS
Kenneth Gatland, FRAS, FBIS
**Illustrated by**
Michael Roffe, Malcolm English
and John Hutchinson
© 1977 Usborne Publishing Ltd.
Published in Australia by
Rigby Ltd., Adelaide, Sydney,
Melbourne, Brisbane and Perth.

**Acknowledgements**
We wish to thank the following
individuals and organizations for
their assistance and for making
available material in their
collections.
Space Frontiers Ltd.
National Aeronautics and Space
Administration (NASA)
British Interplanetary Society
Royal Astronomical Society

First published in 1977 by
Usborne Publishing Ltd.
20 Garrick Street
London WC2E 9BJ
Reprinted 1978
Printed in England by
Waterlow (Dunstable) Ltd.

**On the cover: Viking spacecraft
in orbit above Mars.**

**On this page: The three-star
system of Zeta Cancri.**

# THE EXPERIMENTS

Here is a checklist of the equipment you will need for
the experiments and things to do included in this book.

## WARNING:

**Never look at
the Sun directly, either
with your eyes or through
binoculars or telescopes.
If you want to observe
the Sun, use the safe
Sun-scope shown
on pp. 10–11.**

## General equipment

**Scissors**
**Sticky tape**
**Ruler**
**Chair**
**Binoculars**
**Felt pen and pencil**
If you can afford it, buy a tripod
to mount your binoculars on. Your
arms will not ache, and the view
will be much steadier.

## Special experiments

**Looking at the sky (p.6):**
**Deckchair**
**This book**
**Torch or bicycle lamp**
**Thermos flask**
**Notebook**
**Warm clothing**

**Phases of the Moon (p.8):**
**Grapefruit**
**Golfball**
**Torch**

**Sun-scope (p.10):**
**Two sheets of white card**
**Binoculars**

**Meteorite craters (p.18):**
**Plain white flour**
**Shallow tray**
**Spoon**

**Sky-Spy (p.26):**
**Large sheet of tracing paper**
**A world atlas**
**A sheet of white card**

# WEIGHTS AND MEASURES

All the weights and measures used in this book are Metric.
This list gives some equivalents in Imperial measures.

**mm = millimetre**
**(1 inch = 25.4 mm)**

**cm = centimetre**
**(1 inch = 2.54 cm)**

**m = metre**
**(1 yard = 0.91 m)**

**km = kilometre**
**(1 mile = 1.6 km)**

**kph = kilometres per hour**
**(1,000 mph = 1,609 kph)**

**kps = kilometres per second**

**kg = kilogram**
**(1 pound = 0.45 kg)**

**1 tonne = 1,000 kg**
**(1 ton = 1.02 tonnes)**

**°C = degrees Centigrade**
**(Water freezes at 0°C and boils
at 100°C.)**

**Speed of light = 300,000 kps**
**Light year = 9,460,000 million km**

# The Young Scientist Book of
# STARS & PLANETS

## ABOUT THIS BOOK

**Stars and Planets** is a beginner's guide to the universe we live in. Its clear text and detailed pictures take the reader on a journey through the familiar sights of the night sky and on to the frontiers of the unknown.

**Stars and Planets** explains how scientists think the universe began and how Earth, a speck in space, fits into the cosmic picture. Readers will visit the still smouldering crater of a giant meteor strike, see the planets of the solar system, and be shown how matter and energy are sucked into black holes.

It also contains safe and simple experiments that can be done at home with ordinary household equipment. They range from simple illustrations of scientific principles to projects like building a sun-projector.

## CONTENTS

# THE UNIVERSE OF STARS

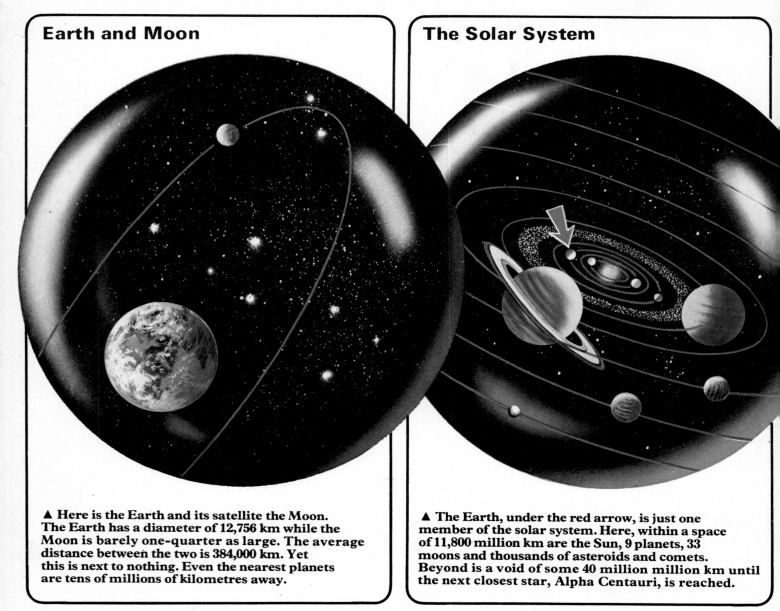

## Earth and Moon

▲ Here is the Earth and its satellite the Moon. The Earth has a diameter of 12,756 km while the Moon is barely one-quarter as large. The average distance between the two is 384,000 km. Yet this is next to nothing. Even the nearest planets are tens of millions of kilometres away.

## The Solar System

▲ The Earth, under the red arrow, is just one member of the solar system. Here, within a space of 11,800 million km are the Sun, 9 planets, 33 moons and thousands of asteroids and comets. Beyond is a void of some 40 million million km until the next closest star, Alpha Centauri, is reached.

The universe is unimaginably huge. Our planet, Earth, is merely a tiny pinpoint in space. As a planet, it is rather small and unimportant. Next to any one of the millions upon millions of stars in the universe, Earth is barely noticeable at all.

In the bubbles above, the red arrows show the location of Earth. Each bubble shows a bigger portion of the universe, the last taking you to the outer limits of known space. Astronomers know that the universe is expanding. How and why this is happening are still very much unanswered questions.

## In the beginning . . .

▲ The origin of the universe has always been a puzzle. Astronomers now favour the 'Big Bang' theory. They think that the universe began about 18,000 million years ago with a colossal explosion.

▼ At the moment of the Bang, all the material in the universe was condensed in a vast 'super atom'. The explosion ripped it apart and scattered dust and gases in every direction.

4

## The Milky Way

▲ The solar system (arrowed) is a minor member of the Milky Way galaxy, a spiral cloud made up of about 180,000 million stars. Distances in deep space are vast so they are measured in light years. One light year is the distance light travels in a year, 9.5 million million km.

## Galaxies like grains of sand

▲ The Milky Way is some 100,000 light years across. Yet it is just one of many millions of galaxies. These galaxies are scattered as far as telescopes can see. They have been spotted up to 8,000 million light years away. Yet the actual size of the universe may be many times larger.

▲ Out of this material the galaxies, stars and planets were formed. But the force of the Bang persists. The universe is still expanding and galaxies everywhere are whizzing apart.

## The expanding universe

In 1842, the Austrian scientist Christian Doppler showed why the sound of approaching and receding objects was different.

Movement causes the sound waves in front of a moving object to be compressed. The ones behind are spaced out.

The Doppler effect also holds true for light. Light waves from a receding star are spaced out, making the light take on a reddish colour. This light change is called the red shift—all the distant galaxies have a red shift, proof that the universe is expanding.

▲ Hear the Doppler effect in action! Look up at a jet plane and note how the sound changes from a high whine to a low roar as it goes overhead. This is the 'sound' version of the red shift.

# LOOKING AT THE SKY

## Two types of telescope

The first telescopes were made in the early 1600s. They were refracting telescopes using lenses to collect light. In 1668, Isaac Newton built the first reflecting telescope. It used a mirror to collect the light.

The large lens in the front of a refracting telescope is called the object glass. It collects light rays and bends (or refracts) them into the telescope's body.

### Refracting telescope

This diagram shows the path of light rays in the telescope.

### Reflecting telescope

This small flat mirror reflects the collected light to the side of the telescope.

The eyepiece picks up the image from the flat mirror. This type of reflector is called the Newtonian focus after its inventor.

The rear lens is called the eyepiece. It magnifies the image for the astronomer to look at.

This diagram shows the path of light rays in the telescope.

The concave mirror collects and reflects light back up the telescope's body.

## All you need to look at the sky

Amateur astronomers can have as much fun as the professionals. You need an atlas of the stars and a pair of binoculars. Even your naked eyes will do as there are over 6,000 stars to be seen this way.

From a comfortable spot outdoors you can chart and log the stars and planets. With luck, you might spot a meteor or comet.

Many comets have been first spotted by amateurs, such as Alcock in 1959 and Ikeya-Seki in 1965.

A comfortable deckchair is the heart of an amateur observatory

You can plot planets and stars with this book

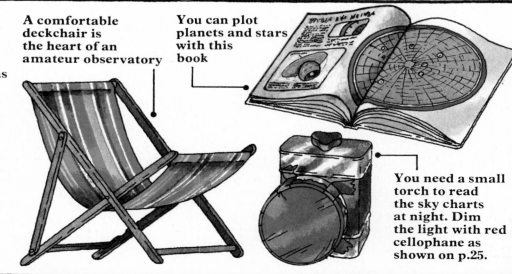

You need a small torch to read the sky charts at night. Dim the light with red cellophane as shown on p.25.

Ever since Galileo turned his telescope to the sky in 1609, astronomers have been improving the instruments with which they study the stars.

Nowadays, most large telescopes are really 'super-cameras' as film is much more sensitive to dim light than the human eye. Special devices help boost the faintest starlight to a clear strong image.

Stars not only give off visible light, but also emit radio and other waves that are invisible to the human eye. Special film is used for photographing them.

▲ The largest optical telescope today is the 6 m reflector at Mount Semirodniki in the Soviet Union, It can gather starlight 10,000 million times fainter than the brightest star in the sky. It could detect a candle 25,000 km away.

## Invisible astronomy

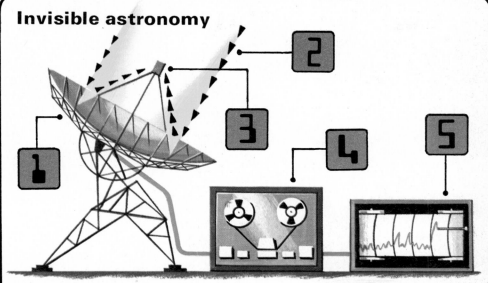

A typical radio telescope has a large bowl-like dish (1). It picks up radio waves from space (2) and focuses them onto a receiver (3). The waves are very feeble when they reach the Earth and so large reflector dishes are needed to collect a recognisable signal. The star signals are recorded on magnetic tape (4) and later fed into a computer which turns them into a graph (5).

▶ Radio telescopes increase the range that astronomers can probe into space. The picture on the right shows the limits of the naked eye and optical and radio telescopes.

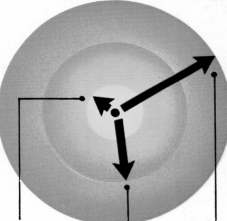

Limits of naked eye       Limits of optical telescopes       Limits of radio telescope

A thermos flask with something hot to drink will keep away the night-time chill.

Use a notepad and pencil to make notes and sketches during your skywatching.

Wear lots of clothes. A pair of old gloves with the fingertips cut off will let you write as well as keep your hands warm.

A good pair of 7 × 50 binoculars is better than a cheap telescope. With these, you should be able to see some of Jupiter's moons and details of lunar craters.

# Friendly Face in the sky—the Moon

**MARE FRIGORIS** Sea of Cold

Aristoteles

Jura Mts

Alp Mts

Luna 17

**MARE IMBRIUM** Sea of Rains

Archimedes

Caucasus Mts

**MARE SERENITATIS** Sea of Serenity

LACUS SOMNIORUM Lake of Dreams

Apollo 15

Apollo 17

Apennine Mts

PALUS SOMNII Marsh of Sleep

**MARE CRISIUM** Sea of Crises

Copernicus

Eratosthenes

**MARE VAPORUM** Sea of Vapours

**MARE TRANQUILLITATIS** Sea of Tranquility

Kepler

OCEANUS PROCELLARUM Ocean of Storms

Apollo 12

Apollo 14

Apollo 11

Luna 20

Luna 16

Ptolemaeus

Apollo 16

**MARE FECUNDITATIS** Sea of Fertility

**MARE NUBIUM** Sea of Clouds

Alphonsus

**MARE NECTARIS** Sea of Nectar

Pyrenee Mts

**MARE HUMORUM** Sea of Moisture

Altai Mts

Langrenus

Tycho

Schickard

Maginus

Clavius

# Phases of the Moon

**1** GRAPE-FRUIT  GOLFBALL  TORCH

**2** GOLFBALL (MOON)  GRAPEFRUIT (EARTH)

**3** POSITION 'A'  SUN'S RAYS

▲ The Moon only shines with reflected sunlight. As it moves around the Earth, we see different parts of its sunny side. For this experiment, you need a torch and two balls— try a golfball and grapefruit.

▲ Balance the torch on a table, or fix it firmly to the back of a chair as shown above. Put the 'Earth' grapefruit and the 'Moon' golfball on the table. Make sure the 'Sun' torch is shining on them both.

▲ Starting from position A shown above, move the Moon around the Earth in a circular orbital path. As the Moon goes around, you will see that the view from Earth goes from shadow to sunlight and then back to shadow again.

# EARTH'S NEAREST NEIGHBOUR

The Moon is our closest companion in space and the only one ever to have been visited by Man. Although it is roughly a quarter the size of Earth, the Moon is far less massive. It would take 81 Moons to make up the same weight as Earth.

Gravity on the Moon is quite feeble—only 1/6th as great as on Earth. It is far too weak to hold an atmosphere. As a result, the Moon is a bleak and arid world where temperatures soar to 100°C by day and plunge to a freezing –130°C at night. The Moon's surface is a monotonous expanse of rock and dust.

3,476 km

12,756 km

▲ To get an idea of the distance between the Earth and Moon, trace off the two scale globes shown above onto a sheet of card. Cut out the two circles and knot a piece of string 1.35 m long between them to see the scale distance.

## The side we never see

Although the Moon spins on its axis, it always keeps the same face to Earth. It takes the Moon as long to rotate once (27.3 days) as it does to circle the Earth. As the direction of rotation and spin are the same, we never see the other side.

Astronomers had the first glimpse of the far side of the Moon in 1959 when the Russian spacecraft Luna 3 passed behind it and took photographs.

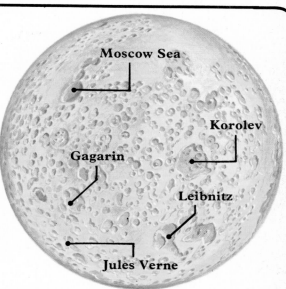

Moscow Sea

Korolev

Gagarin

Leibnitz

Jules Verne

▲ The far side of the Moon is a perfect site for an observatory. Here, optical telescopes would not have to cope with a murky atmosphere. Radio telescopes would use the Moon as a rocky shield 3,500 km thick to protect themselves from the interfering radio waves from Earth. One idea, shown above, is for a vast 'Cyclops-eye' radio telescope to probe into the depths of space.

HOW THE MOON LOOKS AT POSITION 'A'

▲ Put the Moon back at position A again, and peer over the top of the grapefruit Earth. If you have got the angle of the light from the torch right, you should see that the lit portion of the golf-ball Moon looks like a crescent.

WAXING    FULL    WANING

▲ Here are the phases of the Moon as they are seen from Earth. Every 29½ days, the Moon completes a full cycle. It goes through three stages. A waxing Moon is one that is getting larger and brighter. A full Moon is a shining circle in the sky. A waning Moon is getting smaller. When the Moon lies completely in the Sun's shadow, it is known as a new Moon. A crescent Moon in the 'waxing' phase is in the same place as position A in your small-scale experiment model.

# THE NEAREST STAR

The Sun is just an ordinary star. The only reason it looks like a huge burning ball in the sky is that it is millions of times closer to Earth than any other star.

The Sun is the source of all life on Earth. The nuclear reactions in its core provide a steady stream of life-giving light and heat. The Earth receives barely 1/2000 millionth of the total radiation of the Sun. Yet this is enough to warm the planet and provide all the energy for plant and animal life.

Though the Sun uses up four million tonnes of fuel every second, it has enough to burn for a good 6,000 million years yet.

▲ The German-built, American-launched Helios probe was sent up in December 1974 to study the Sun at close range. Its nearest approach was to within 37 million km.

At times, long looping streams of gas called prominences arch up from the Sun. They climb into space at speeds up to 600 kps. Small short-lived prominences are called spicules

Size of Earth to scale

Dark patches on the Sun's surface are sunspots. They are 1000–2000° C cooler than the surface and so shine less brightly. Sunspots usually appear in pairs. They develop in a few hours and may last for many months.

The surface of the Sun is in continuous upheaval. Swirling gas eruptions called flares often occur with sunspot formations. They release bursts of intense radiation causing magnetic storms that disrupt radio communication on Earth.

## DANGER—DO NOT LOOK AT THE SUN

Never, ever, look at the Sun through binoculars, telescopes, or even just with your eyes. The strong light can easily blind you. Even smoked glass and sun filters should never be used as they do not block out all the dangerous rays.

## Make a safe Sunscope

▲ It is very dangerous to look at the Sun. Filters exist that screen out harmful rays, but it is easier and cheaper to make this sunscope. You need a pair of binoculars — 7 × 50 are ideal — and two sheets of stiff white card.

▲ You need a square of card about 40 cm × 40 cm. Cut a hole in it as shown above, just big enough to fit one of the binocular lenses. The other lens will not be used in the Sunscope, so you only need the one hole.

**Temperatures at the core of the Sun rise to an incredible 14 million°C.**

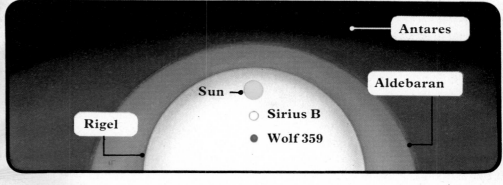

Antares

Aldebaran

Sun →

Sirius B

Rigel

Wolf 359

▲ The Sun has a diameter of about 1.4 million km. Its interior could hold more than a million planets the size of Earth. Although this flaming ball of gases looks like the biggest thing in the sky, it is in fact merely a medium-sized yellow star orbiting far out in one of the spiralling arms of an average sized galaxy. The picture above shows the Sun compared with some of its stellar neighbours. As you can see, it is a very ordinary star indeed.

The corona is the outer part of the Sun's atmosphere. It can best be seen during a total eclipse when it looks like a glowing halo around the Sun.

The Sun's surface is called the photosphere. Here, the temperature is about 6000°C. Immediately above it is the chromosphere, a thin layer of gases where temperatures fall to 4500°C.

Surrounding the burning core is a radiation zone of tremendously hot gases. They transmit radiation from the core to the surface.

▲ This picture shows a total eclipse of the Sun. From time to time the Moon passes in front of it and exactly covers the Sun's disc. This is the only time the shining halo of the corona can be seen.

TAPE

▲ Lay the card on a table and balance the binoculars on it, making sure that one lens fits over the hole you have cut. Carefully tape the binoculars into place. They must be firm so do not skimp on the tape!

SUN'S IMAGE

WHITE CARD

▲ For a screen you need a large sheet of white card. Prop it against a chair at right-angles to the Sun in the sky. Focus the binoculars on infinity and hold them in front of the card. The Sun should appear on it.

THE SUN

SUNSPOTS

▲ This is the sort of image you should get quite easily. Move the binoculars backwards and forwards until the image is sharp. With luck, you will see some tiny black specks on the Sun—they are sunspots.

**TAKE CARE—if you adjust the Sun's image to make a pinpoint, you may burn the card.**

Sun

Mercury

Venus

Earth

Mars

Asteroids

Comets

Jupiter

Saturn

# FAMILY OF THE SUN

The solar system consists of the entire family of planets, moons, asteroids, comets, meteors and swirling dust and gases that circles the Sun. The Sun itself is more than 750 times as massive as the rest of the system combined. Its enormous pull of gravity locks everything within a range of over 6000 million kilometres into orbit around it.

After the Sun, the most important members of the solar system are the nine planets. The chart below shows you some of the more important facts about each one. Planets' 'days' and 'years' vary because they spin at different speeds and move along in their orbits at varying rates. Pluto, for instance, rotates every 153 hours compared with Earth's rotation time of 23 hours 56 minutes, so Pluto's day is more than six times longer than Earth's.

## Facts and figures

| Name of planet | Diameter in km | Average distance from Sun in million km | Number of moons | Time taken to go around the Sun (year) | Time taken to turn on its axis (day) | Speed in orbit around the Sun in kps |
|---|---|---|---|---|---|---|
| Mercury | 4,900 | 57.8 | — | 88 days | 59 days | 47.9 |
| Venus | 12,200 | 108 | — | 224.7 days | 243 days | 35 |
| Earth | 12,756 | 149.7 | 1 | 365.3 days | 23 hours 56 mins | 29.8 |
| Mars | 6,780 | 227.8 | 2 | 687 days | 24 hours 37.5 mins | 24.1 |
| Jupiter | 142,900 | 779 | 13 | 11.9 years | 9 hours 50.5 mins | 13.1 |
| Saturn | 120,050 | 1,430 | 10 | 29.5 years | 10 hours 14 mins | 9.6 |
| Uranus | 49,000 | 2,868 | 5 | 84 years | 10 hours 50 mins | 6.8 |
| Neptune | 47,000 | 4,508 | 2 | 164.8 years | 15 hours 50 mins | 5.4 |
| Pluto | 5,800 | 5,908 | — | 247.7 years | 6 days 9 hours | 4.8 |

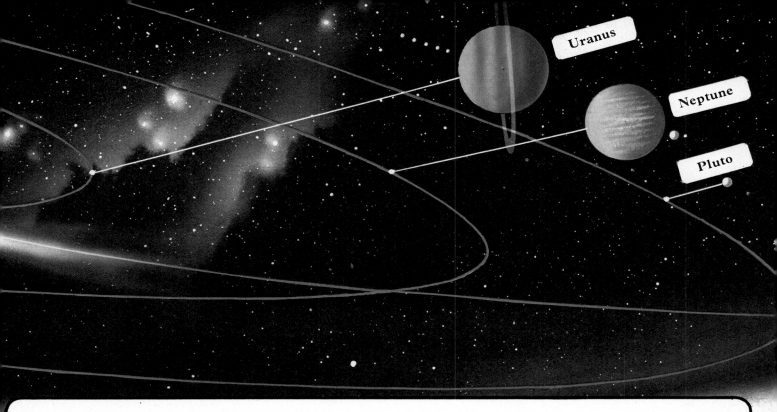

Uranus

Neptune

Pluto

## Plotting the planets

The Planets swing around the Sun in regular orbits. From Earth, they seem to move across a narrow belt of sky. This is because the planets circle the Sun in a roughly flat plane, rather like the bands between tracks on an LP record. The only exception is frozen Pluto, the outermost planet which has an angled orbital path.

The planets move through twelve star constellations called the signs of the Zodiac. Once you have spotted the constellations, any extra 'star' will be a planet. The chart below shows where you can see the four brightest planets during the next few years.

Key to the planetary symbols shown below

♀ Venus   ♃ Jupiter

♂ Mars   ♄ Saturn

# THE INNER PLANETS

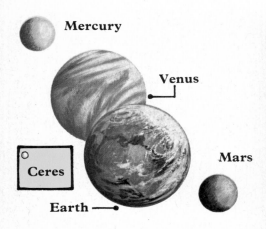

Mercury

Venus

Ceres

Mars

Earth

The four inner planets are the midgets of the solar system. The diagram above shows them all to the same scale, together with Ceres, the biggest asteroid. All are quite dense and, apart from Earth, have barren, rocky surfaces. The features of Earth are softened by the great oceans that cover 71% of its surface.

Only the thinnest of atmospheres exist on Mercury and Mars. As a result there is a great difference between day and night-time temperatures. On Mercury the change can be as high as 600°C. Earth and Venus, however, have shielding atmospheres. Their temperatures are fairly constant. On Earth at the equator, this is about 15°C while most of Venus roasts at nearly 500°C — hot enough to melt lead!

▲ Tiny Mercury is the nearest planet to the Sun which, looming some three times as big as it does on Earth, sears the landscape to a baking 400°C.
In 1974, Mariner 10 passed the planet and snapped the first detailed pictures. They showed a dry rocky surface that was scarred with craters. Instruments on board showed Mercury to have a dense iron-rich core much like that of Earth's.

▲ Venus, the morning and evening 'star', ought to be Earth's sister planet. Its size is almost identical, yet it is a hell-world shrouded by clouds of sulphuric acid and smothered by an atmosphere of carbon dioxide.

Light from Sun

Atmosphere of Venus

Cloud layer

−35°C

235°C

477°C

Heat trapped here

Surface of Venus

▲ The clouds that blanket Venus trap sunlight like a greenhouse. Light passes through the clouds and heats the surface. The ground radiates infra-red heat waves that are trapped by the atmosphere making temperatures soar.

▲ From nearby space, Earth shines like a blue-white beacon in the sky. Even from the Moon, the brown outlines of the continents, the deep blue of the oceans and the white swirls of the clouds can be clearly seen.

▲ In 1976 two space probes, Vikings 1 and 2, soft-landed on Mars and sent back the first surface pictures. The view above was taken by Viking 2. The horizon is about 3 km away. The fine drifting sand is the result of storms that can rage across Mars.

## Lost planet?

Orbiting in the 550 million km gap between Mars and Jupiter are tens of thousands of small rocky objects called asteroids. Ceres, the biggest, is only 760 km across—most are only house or boulder-sized. Some astronomers think they may be the remains of a tiny planet which broke up into pieces.

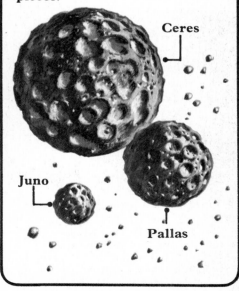

Ceres

Juno

Pallas

▲ This picture shows the largest moon of Mars, Phobos, as it might appear from the viewport of a visiting spacecraft as it approaches the red planet. To give you an idea of the moon's size, the crater in the middle is 6 km across. Phobos orbits 6000 km above Mars, circling it three times every Martian day. The other moon of Mars, Deimos, is even smaller than Phobos. It must appear as little more than a bright moving star from the surface.

15

# THE OUTER PLANETS

Beyond the Asteroid Belt are the outer giants—Jupiter, Saturn, Uranus and Neptune—vast balls of gas circling in the solar system's outer reaches. Beyond them all lies tiny frozen Pluto.

The diagram below compares Earth and the outer planets shown to the same scale.

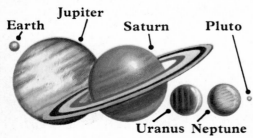

Earth  Jupiter  Saturn  Pluto

Uranus  Neptune

▲ Jupiter is the Goliath of the solar system. It has a volume 1,312 times that of Earth and contains two and a half times as much material as all the other planets put together. Jupiter does not have a solid surface. Its upper layers are a sea of gases that become a denser liquid and finally a solid near the core. In the gaseous cloud layer, temperatures average 140°C.

The oddest feature is the Great Red Spot (shown on the right in the picture above), first seen in 1631. Astronomers think it may be a long-lasting storm raging in the planet's atmosphere.

Jupiter is surrounded by strong radiation belts. They nearly ruined the instruments of Pioneer 10 (shown above) in 1973.

Saturn

Earth

▲ ▼ Saturn, with its halo of beautiful rings, orbits 1,430 million km from the Sun. It is a gas-giant like Jupiter, but its amazing rings

▲ Uranus is an icy world 2,868 million km from the Sun. Latest studies show that in addition to its five moons (two of which are passing in front of it in the picture above), it has a ring of tiny moonlets–just like Saturn's.

▲ Neptune is the last of the giant planets. It is similar to Uranus but slightly smaller in size. Its two moons are named Triton and Nereid. Its surface has been calculated to be at a constant and chilly −220°C.

are what make it really interesting. The rings, which are barely 15 km thick, are not solid since starlight shines through them. They are made up of rock and ice pieces—the remains, perhaps, of a moon which got too close to Saturn and broke up into billions of fragments.

The picture above shows how the rings might look from close-up as a 21st century survey craft edges its way slowly into them on an exploration mission.

From Earth, the rings look different from year to year as the planet whirls around in its orbit. The pictures below show how the view changes. From being almost invisible when the rings are seen edge-on, they swing into view as a splendid grandstand panorama.

Saturn is made mainly from the light gases hydrogen and helium. If you could place it in water, Saturn would float!

Arrows show position of Pluto

▲ Pluto, at the boundary of the solar system, was not discovered until 1930. Photographs taken on different nights were compared using a device called a blink comparator. One of the 'stars'— Pluto—moved from night to night.

# METEORS AND COMETS

Along with the planets and moons, a great deal of space debris circles the Sun. Most of it is too tiny and distant to be seen from Earth, but at times some of these objects become spectacularly visible.

The smallest are the meteoroids which range from tiny specks to boulder size. They can be seen only when they hurtle into the atmosphere as streaks of light called shooting stars.

Comets are solitary wanderers. A long shining tail announces their arrival whenever they drift in from space and near the Sun.

▲ The picture above shows a meteor as it streaks into the Earth's atmosphere at a speed up to 70 kps. Friction with the air vapourizes most meteors before they get anywhere near the Earth's surface.

▶ Giant meteorites hitting the Earth are very rare, although thousands of tiny meteors burn up in the atmosphere every day. This picture shows what the scene might be like a short time after a huge meteorite hit. Scientists in helicopters hover over and in the newly gouged crater. Luckily, it is in a deserted area.

## Meteorite craters

Astronomers call meteors different names according to where they are. A chunk of rock or stone in space is a meteoroid. The same chunk is called a meteor as it falls through the atmosphere. If it actually hits the Earth (or any planet or satellite such as the Moon), it is called a meteorite.

Meteorites can either land in one piece or they can explode violently. In 1947, a thousand tonnes of exploding meteorite fragments rained down on Siberia digging craters up to 30 m wide.

▲ It is easy to make your own meteorite crater with this simple experiment. The surface of your model planet is a bed of flour. Cover the bottom of a shallow tray with a layer of fine plain flour about 2 cm thick.

▲ Smooth off the flour with the edge of a ruler. It is important to have a smooth even surface for the experiment to be a success. Place the tray on the floor. Now cover the floor with newspaper for the next step.

## Comets—dirty snowballs in space

Comets appear from the depths of space as glowing balls with million km tails. A comet's nucleus is a ball of solid particles and frozen ices enveloped by a coma of evaporating gases. A nucleus a few km wide may have a coma of 80,000 km. The Sun's heat and radiation boils away the gas particles from the coma and spreads them back to form a long filmy tail stretching into space.

Tail made of gases and dust    Gaseous coma    Nucleus made of rocks and ice

Path of Halley's Comet

1948

1980

1985

1986

1987

It orbits the Sun once every 76 years

Tail is formed as it nears the Sun

Tail always points away from the Sun

**3** ABOUT 2 m    MAKE SURE YOU CLEAN THE FLOOR!

▲ Climb up on a chair so you are standing directly above the tray. Take a small spoonful of flour, hold it about 2 m above the floor and let the flour drop. Repeat the experiment a few times from different heights.

**4** RAISED CRATER RIM

▲ The flour ploughs into the tray just like a meteorite hitting the Earth or Moon. You will see that all the mini-craters that are formed in your tray have the same sort of raised lip and sloping sides as real craters.

**5** CRATER    METEORITE    SHATTERED ROCK

▲ The largest meteorite crater on Earth was formed 50,000 years ago in the Arizona desert. An iron-nickel meteorite some 80 m wide, blasted into the Earth. It gouged a hole out that was 1,265 m wide and 175 m deep.

# STAR-SPOTTING IN THE NORTHERN SKY

There are about 6,000 stars in the night sky that can be seen by the naked eye. Not all are visible at once as only a small part of the heavens can be seen from any single place on Earth.

The brightest stars can be made out on their own, but others are more easily recognised as parts of constellations. These are groups of stars that seem to form patterns. They were well-known to ancient peoples who thought that the stars were arranged in the forms of animals, mythical creatures and men. There are 88 constellations. The Plough, in Ursa Major, is one of the easiest to spot.

▲ You need the Sky-Spy shown on pp.26–27 if you want to use the sky charts properly. Simply line up the time on the Sky-Spy with the date on the chart. The view inside the oval is what you will be able to see on that night in the sky.

▶ Here are the main constellations of the northern sky. The big numbers on this map link with the pictures on the next two pages.

## Mapping the heavens

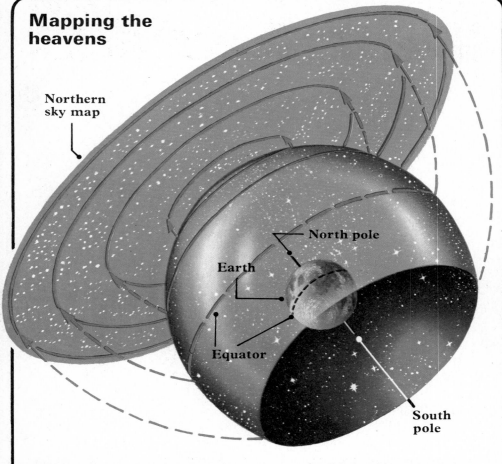

Northern sky map

North pole

Earth

Equator

South pole

**Stars look as though they have been painted on a dark dome.** It used to be thought that the stars lay in fixed positions on the inside surface of a hollow globe—the celestial sphere—with the Earth sitting at its centre. The star maps in this book are made by 'folding back' the view seen from Earth to make a flat circle. So, although there is no real celestial sphere, the idea can still be used to make accurate maps of the sky.

# WONDERS OF THE NORTHERN SKY

Not only stars and planets can be seen in the night sky, but also dark nebulae, star clusters, galaxies and shining clouds of heated gas. Many of these sights are too faint to be spotted unaided. They are only visible with powerful telescopes.

All objects in the sky are ranked according to their brightness. This is called their order of magnitude. Curiously, bright objects are given low numbers; Venus for example is −4.4. Dim objects have high numbers. The faintest object you can see unaided is around magnitude +6.

▲ Our own galaxy, the Milky Way, looks like a dim trail of light stretching across the sky. Pictures like the one above show it to be made up of millions of stars so thickly sprinkled that they look like clouds.

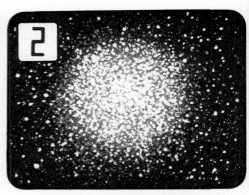

▲ The fuzzy patch in Hercules called M13 is a tight globular star cluster. Here, hundreds of thousands of old dim yellow stars are crowded together. They are packed less than half a light year apart.

▲ The Pleiades are a compact group of stars in the constellation Taurus. They are about 370 light years away. The Pleiades are also known as the 'Seven Sisters' since most people can only see seven stars here. However, on a clear night and with very good eyesight, others come into view. Only the sharpest eyes can make out more than fifteen, yet in actual fact there are nearly 400. North American Indians used the Pleiades as a way of testing the keenness of a warrior's eyesight.

The blue-white stars in the Pleiades are 'young'—just a few tens of millions of years old. The Sun is 5,000 million years old in contrast.

▲ With the Plough as a guide, draw an imaginary line along the curve of its handle. If you continue the line in the same path, it will cross Arcturus, the brightest star to be seen in the northern sky.

▲ The constellation Orion can be seen in both northern and southern skies. The picture above shows you how to find Betelgeuse at its top left-hand corner. Betelgeuse is a red-giant star 30 million times larger than the Sun.

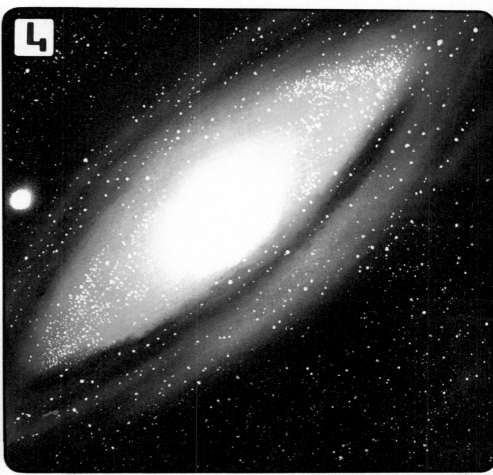

▲ This picture shows the most distant object which can be seen with the naked eye—the Andromeda galaxy. It looks like a faint smudge. It was thought to be a nebula, a cloud of gas and dust, until the astronomer Edwin Hubble measured its distance in 1923. It turned out to be about two million light years away. Its shape is very like that of our own Milky Way galaxy, complete with arms made of billions of stars spiralling out from the galactic centre.

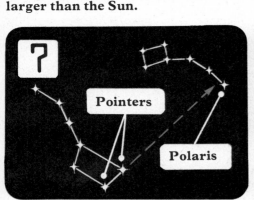

▲ The seven brightest stars of the constellation Ursa Major are called the Plough. A line between the two end stars, the Pointers, runs straight to Polaris when extended upwards. Face Polaris and you always face north.

▲ Stars seem to be fixed in the sky. Yet with enough time, movements do become apparent. 100,000 years ago, the stars of the Plough were an unrecognizable jumble. Today, their familiar form is easy to see. In another 100,000 years, the shape will be transformed yet again.

Although stars move at high speeds, they are so far away that any motion is impossible to make out, except with high precision instruments.

► The big numbers on this map link with the picture opposite and with the pictures on the following pages.

FEBRUARY

MARCH

Late
Middle
Early

Early
Middle
Late

JANUARY

Late
Middle
Early

HERCULES

MILKY WAY

CORONA BOREALIS

SERPENS

CYGNUS
SAGITTA
DELPHINUS

OPHIUCHUS

Sabik

Altair

AQUILA

SCORPIUS

LIBRA

Spica

CORVUS

DECEMBER

Late
Early

SAGITTARIUS

CAPRICORNUS

ARA

LUPUS

HYDRA

AQUARIUS

PISCIS AUSTRINUS

Fomalhaut

SCULPTOR

GRUS

TRIANGULUM AUSTRALE

AUSTRALE

CENTAURUS

November
Middle

PEGASUS

PHOENIX

Achernar

Small Magellanic Cloud

Large Magellanic Cloud

OCTANS

**5**

**2**

CRUX

VELA

CARINA

Early

PISCES

CETUS

ERIDANUS

Canopus

CANIS MAJOR

Sirius

MONOCEROS

**3**

**1**

**4**

OCTOBER

Late
Middle
Early

ARIES
TRIANGULUM

Rigel

Betelgeuse

ORION

TAURUS
Aldebaran

CANIS MINOR

GEMINI

Late
Middle
Early

SEPTEMBER

Early
Late

AUGUST
Middle
Early

24

# STAR-SPOTTING IN THE SOUTHERN SKY

You will not see most of the stars shown on this map unless you live in the same latitude as Buenos Aires, Sydney or Cape Town. But the stars along the outer edges of this map overlap onto the northern map as well, and at certain times of the year, they can be seen low on the horizon in the north.

Astronomers still identify stars by a system first used in 1603. The brightest star in each constellation is called Alpha—the Greek A. The next brightest is Beta, the second letter, and so on. Alpha Centauri, therefore, is the brightest star in Centaurus.

STICK ON RED MASK WITH TAPE

▲ You will need a nightlight to read with whenever you take your sky map outside to go star spotting. So that the glare does not spoil your night vision, take along a torch masked with red cellophane.

## Wonders of the southern sky

Because the southern sky was neglected for so long, a number of surprises awaited astronomers when they directed their attentions here. In the constellation Centaurus they found our closest stellar neighbour. Proxima Centauri is a small dim red star just 4.24 light years away. Here in the south are also the nearest galaxies, called the Magellanic Clouds after their discoverer, Ferdinand Magellan.

▲ Hanging near the three stars forming the 'belt' of Orion is one of the most magnificent sights in the sky. To the naked eye, the Great Nebula is a faint fuzzy patch. Seen through a telescope, as shown in the picture above, it leaps into view as a vast and colourful cloud of gas 16 light years across.

The young hot stars embedded in the cloud radiate 8 times as brightly as the Sun. They make the billowing clouds of surrounding gas heat up and shine as well.

▲ The Southern Cross, shown in close-up above, is a tiny constellation, the smallest in the sky. Two of its member stars point toward the south, just as two of The Plough's stars point north toward Polaris.

▲ Dark nebulae are clouds of cold dust and gases. They can only be seen when they blot out part of a lighter background of stars. The Horsehead Nebula in Orion, shown above, stands out in silhouette against the bright stars behind.

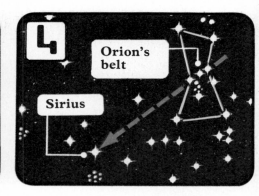

▲ Sirius is the brightest star in the southern night sky. It is also known as the Dog Star because it lies in the constellation Canis Major, the Great Dog. The picture above shows you how to find Sirius using Orion's Belt as a guide.

# PLANS FOR YOUR SKY-SPY

This simple gadget will show you which stars can be seen from your home at any particular time of the year.

Get a large sheet of tracing paper and lay it over this page. Trace off the solid black lines from the yellow half-plan on the right. Now mark on the time arrows from midnight to 6 am.

Flip the tracing paper over. Trace out the other half of the plan. Mark on the evening time arrows from midnight to 6 pm. Also trace on the star where the vertical and horizontal lines cross.

Slide the star on your tracing paper along the degrees of latitude scale until it rests on your own latitude. You can find the latitude of your home in an atlas.

Here are some examples:

| | |
|---|---|
| Copenhagen | 56°North |
| London | 52°North |
| Munich | 48°North |
| Rome | 42°North |
| Rio de Janeiro | 23°South |
| Sydney | 34°South |

Now trace out the dotted oval of the horizon line. As you can see, the oval moves north or south depending on where you live.

Transfer your finished tracing onto a sheet of stiff card cut out to the same shape. Lastly, cut out the oval centre. Your Sky-Spy is now complete.

MIDNIGHT

MORNING TIME ARROWS

STAR

EVENING TIME ARROWS

TRACING PAPER

12 MID-NIGHT
1 A.M.
2 A.M.
3 A.M.
4 A.M.

EVENING    MORNING

FINISHED SKY-SPY ON CARD

OVAL HOLE TO SEE WHICH STARS ARE IN THE SKY

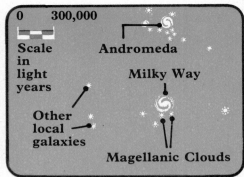

▲ The Magellanic Clouds were first noted in 1519. They are visible only in the southern sky. The Large Cloud, also known by its scientific name Nubecula Major, is shown in the picture above. It is 170,000 light years away from the Milky Way making it the nearest galaxy to us, almost a satellite in fact. It is 23,000 light years across. Unlike spiral and disc-shaped galaxies, the clouds have no particular shape or form. They are classed as irregular galaxies.

▲ The Magellanic Clouds and 20 other galaxies belong to the Local Group. This cluster of galaxies (of which the Milky Way is a member) lies within a 5 million light year diameter sphere. Other clusters can contain up to 2,500 galaxies.

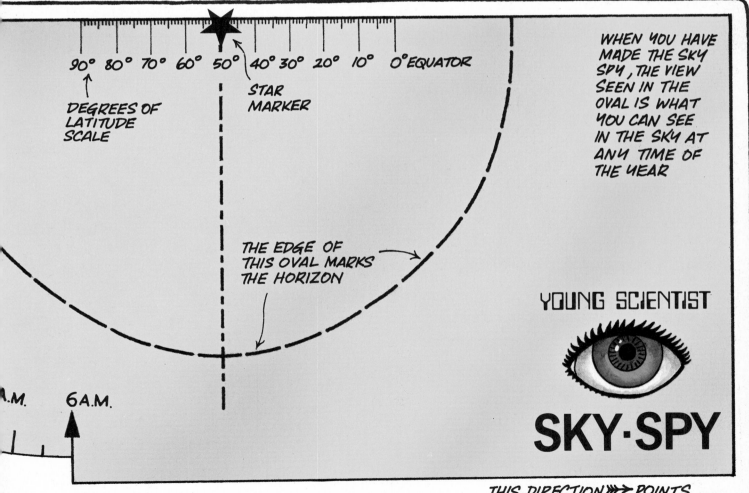

90° 80° 70° 60° 50° 40° 30° 20° 10° 0° EQUATOR

DEGREES OF LATITUDE SCALE

STAR MARKER

THE EDGE OF THIS OVAL MARKS THE HORIZON

WHEN YOU HAVE MADE THE SKY SPY, THE VIEW SEEN IN THE OVAL IS WHAT YOU CAN SEE IN THE SKY AT ANY TIME OF THE YEAR

A.M.   6 A.M.

YOUNG SCIENTIST

SKY·SPY

THIS DIRECTION ⫸ POINTS NORTH IF YOU LIVE IN EARTH'S NORTHERN HEMISPHERE. IT POINTS SOUTH IF YOU LIVE IN THE SOUTHERN HEMISPHERE.

# OTHER THINGS TO SEE

## Meteors

At regular times of the year, swarms of meteors cross the Earth's orbit. A heavy meteor shower looks like lots of streaks of light coming from a point in the sky—the radiant.

| Name of shower | Where to look | When to look |
|---|---|---|
| Aquarids | SW of Pegasus | May 4–6 |
| Geminids | Castor in Gemini | December 10–13 |
| Leonids | Leo | November 16–18 |
| Lyrids | Between Hercules and Vega | April 20–22 |
| Orionids | Between Orion and Gemini | October 18–22 |
| Perseids | Perseus | August 10–12 |
| Quadran—tids | Between Böotes and Draco | January 1–3 |
| Taurids | Between Taurus and Perseus | November 5–9 |

## Man-made satellites

Some of the most successful satellites have been the orbiting astronomical observatories such as HEAO-1 shown here. It was launched to study X-ray and other high energy sources in outer space. Its findings have contributed directly to the discovery of black holes.
Since the USSR launched Sputnik 1 in 1957, over 2,100 other satellites have followed it into the sky. Sputnik 1 was just 58 cm wide and weighed only 84 kg. Today's satellites can weigh many tonnes.

## Comets

Comets travel in long swooping orbits that may take them far into the outer reaches of the solar system. It can be hundreds, even thousands of years before they return.

ENCKE'S: Appears at a regular interval of 3.3 years. This small comet swings as far as Jupiter before turning back to the Sun.

HALLEY'S: Shown above, this comet returns every 76 years. It is next due in 1986. Records of its arrival go back over 2,000 years.

HUMASON 1961E: Discovered in 1961, this large comet has a long flat orbit that takes thousands of years to complete. It is next expected in the year 4860

IKEYA-SEKI: Discovered in 1965 by two amateur astronomers, this bright comet could be seen even in daytime.

## Eclipses

Solar eclipses can be predicted years ahead as the globes and chart show. Eclipse paths race across the face of the Earth at speeds of 1,700 kph.

| 1 | October 12, 1977 |
|---|---|
| 2 | February 26, 1979 |
| 3 | February 16, 1980 |
| 4 | July 31, 1981 |
| 5 | June 11, 1983 |
| 6 | November 12, 1985 |
| 7 | November 22–23, 1984 |
| 8 | October 3, 1986 |
| 9 | March 8, 1988 |
| 10 | July 22, 1990 |

# STRANGE FRONTIERS

Recently discovered objects in space seem to disobey the laws of nature. Astronomers know that gravity is one of the weakest forces in the universe. Yet they were astonished to find that it can sometimes make matter and energy apparently vanish.

A place where this occurs is called a black hole. In this region, the forces of gravity are so intense that anything which comes near is sucked inside. Even light rays cannot escape its clutches, so a black hole is completely invisible!

## Birth of a black hole

**Black holes are the result of a process called gravitational collapse. The atoms of a star are squeezed closer and closer to each other so that the star gets ever more dense—a little like the difference between say, balsa wood and lead. One way in which this could happen is when a giant star, shown on the right, explodes violently.**

**The outer layers of the star are flung off into space. If there is enough material left in the core, it collapses inward to form a small super-dense globe called a neutron star. A single matchbox of it would weigh 100 million tonnes. As a neutron star spins, it beams out rapid bursts of radiation (the wavy lines in the picture) to the universe.**

**Some neutron stars shrink still further to become black holes. A black hole is an odd object—infinitely small, yet infinitely dense! The picture below shows how a black hole bends the fabric of space creating a sort of 'plug-hole' effect. Anything falling inside it is likely, as far as astronomers can tell, to be completely crushed or sucked right out of our universe.**

## A world the size of a pea!

**If the Earth were crushed as much as the matter inside a black hole, it would fit inside a sphere the size of a pea. From where you read these words, the force of the black hole's gravity would pull you to pieces and swallow you into the page.**

# SKY FIRSTS

Hundreds of notable landmarks lie scattered through the history of astronomy. Below are just a very few.

**140 AD**
**Ptolemy of Alexandria wrote the Almagest, recording all the astronomical knowledge of the ancient world. He also produced the most accurate star catalogue of his time.**

**1054 AD**
**Chinese astronomers recorded a supernova explosion in Taurus. The Crab Nebula is the remnant of this event.**

**1543**
**Copernicus laid the groundwork of modern astronomy by showing that the Earth and all the planets revolved around the Sun.**

Isaac Newton's reflecting telescope

**1608**
**The Dutchman, Hans Lippershey, used the magnifying power of glass lenses to build the first telescope. The following year, Galileo used his own telescope to observe sunspots, the moons of Jupiter and the stars of the Milky Way.**

**1668**
**The first telescopes were crude refractors. In 1668, Newton invented the reflecting telescope. Though only 16 cm long, it was as powerful as a 200 cm refractor.**

**1705**
**Edmund Halley discovered that comets have regular orbits. He correctly predicted the return of 'Halley's Comet' in 1758.**

**1801**
**Guiseppe Piazzi discovered Ceres, the largest of all the asteroids.**

**1905**
**Albert Einstein proposed the first of his theories of relativity and changed the way we think about the universe. He linked the ideas of space (height, width, length) and time to explain how the universe worked.**

**1937**
**Grote Reber built the first true radio telescope. He set up a 9 m reflecting dish in his garden to study the radio noises that came from the sky.**

**1960**
**Radio astronomers discover quasars (quasi-stellar radio sources). These puzzling objects lie at tremendous distances from us—as much as 15,000 million light years away. They are a fraction the size of galaxies yet hundreds of times brighter.**

**1967**
**Unexpected signals from space were discovered by astronomers at Cambridge, England. These unknown pulses turned out to be coming from rapidly spinning neutron stars. They were called pulsars. One has been found in the middle of the Crab Nebula, right at the heart of the supernova explosion of 1054.**

Crab Nebula

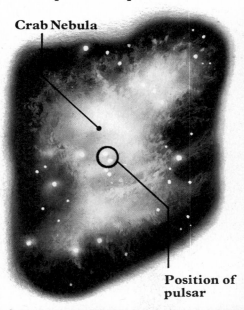

Position of pulsar

# SKY FACTS

Men have been studying the night sky for centuries yet it never ceases to yield new secrets.

In the last 40 years, radio astronomy has opened up a new side of the universe. Astronomers no longer study only visible light. They can now explore nearly the whole spectrum of radiation. Their findings are proving to be more spectacular than anyone could have imagined.

**Here is a list of the ten brightest stars you can see in the sky.**

| Name | Constellation |
| --- | --- |
| Sirius | Canis Major |
| Canopus | Carina |
| Alpha Centauri | Centaurus |
| Arcturus | Bootes |
| Vega | Lyra |
| Capella | Auriga |
| Rigel | Orion |
| Procyon | Canis Major |
| Achernar | Eridanus |
| Beta Centauri | Centaurus |

**Although the face of Venus is hidden by an unbroken layer of cloud, the surface is not so dark as was expected. The USSR landed Venus 9 and 10 successfully in 1975. The probes sent back pictures that show the surface to be no gloomier than an overcast day time scene on Earth. Venusian clouds proved to be more like a haze than a blanket.**

**Quasars are some of the most energetic objects in the sky. They seem to be radiating the energy of 100,000 million Suns from compact areas not much bigger than our own solar system. They may be galaxies being destroyed by massive explosions at their centre. They are also the most distant objects yet discovered. On average they lie some 10,000 million light years away.**

The Sun shivers, but not with cold. Astronomers have recently detected wobbling movements that make the Sun larger or smaller by up to 10 km. These jelly-like vibrations last no more than a few hours at a time. At present, astronomers have no idea what causes them.

Pluto seems to be a 'shrinking' planet. Latest measurements show it to be only 3,500–4,000 km in diameter. If this is true, it will replace Mercury as the smallest planet of all. Because of its strange orbit, Pluto will be closer to the Sun than Neptune between 1979 and 1999.

Astronomers estimate that there could be up to 10 million black holes in the Milky Way galaxy.

Time-exposure photograph of a man-made satellite passing overhead. If you see one, it will look like a bright moving star.

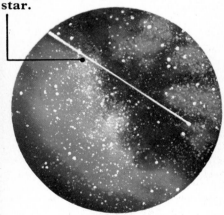

On October 4, 1957, the first man-made satellite was launched. Since Sputnik I, over 1,600 other space launches have been made. All in all, the number of rockets, satellites and other bits of debris littering space total more than 9,000. Roughly 5,000 of these have either fallen back to Earth or landed on the Moon, on Mars or on Venus. About 3,650 objects are still swooping around our planet and can often be spotted at night. The rest are drifting around the Sun, the Moon and the other planets.

# SKY WORDS

This glossary includes words that are not fully explained elsewhere in the book.

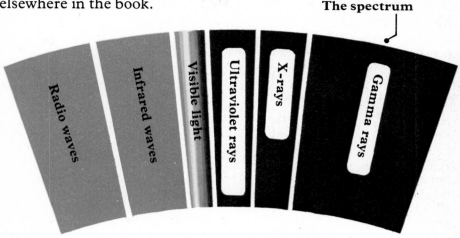

The spectrum

Radio waves
Infrared waves
Visible light
Ultraviolet rays
X-rays
Gamma rays

**Astronomical unit (AU)**
The average distance from the Sun to the Earth (150 million km) is an astronomical unit. It is a shorthand way of measuring distances within the solar system.

**Big bang**
Theory which holds that the entire universe began as a vast 'super-atom' of matter and energy that exploded, (the Bang), and sent all the galaxies hurtling through space.

**Binary**
Two stars in the same sun-system revolving around each other. Three, four and even more stars can link together like this.

**Constellation**
Group of stars seeming to make a shape or pattern in the sky.

**Cosmic rays**
Ultra high speed atomic particles that come shooting to Earth from outer space and from the Sun.

**Galaxy**
Stars are not randomly sprinkled throughout the universe. They are grouped in great clouds or galaxies. Each one contains thousands of millions of stars.

**Gravity**
The force of attraction that exists between one heavenly body and another. The more massive an object, the greater its gravity.

**Light year**
The distance light travels in a year (9,460,000 million km).

**Magnitude**
The brightness of a star or other object shining in space.

**Orbit**
The path of one body as it moves around another one in space. The pull of gravity keeps objects in orbit.

**Radiation**
Light, radio waves and any other form of energy is known as radiation.

**Red shift**
When the light of a star shifts to the red end of the spectrum, the star is receding from us. This is an example of the Doppler Effect.

**Satellite**
Smaller objects which revolve around a larger one and are held by its gravity are called satellites. The Moon is a satellite of Earth.

**Spectrum**
Visible light is one kind of radiation. Radio waves, infrared, ultraviolet and X-rays are other kinds. The entire range of radiation is called the spectrum. Visible light takes up a very small slot somewhere in the middle.

**Solar wind**
Clouds of atomic particles streaming away from the Sun at high speed.

# INDEX

# GOING FURTHER

## Organizations

**British Astronomical Association**
**Burlington House**
**London, W.1**

**British Interplanetary Society**
**12 Bessborough Gardens**
**London, SW1**

**Junior Astronomical Society**
**58 Vaughan Gardens**
**Ilford, Essex**

**Royal Astronomical Society**
**Burlington House**
**London, W1**

## Books to read

**Answer Book of Astronomy**
**by Iain Nicolson**
**Hamlyn, 1975**

**Asimov on Astronomy**
**by Isaac Asimov**
**Macdonald & Jane's, 1974**

**The Next Ten Thousand Years**
**by Adrian Berry**
**Coronet, 1976**

**Challenge of the Stars**
**by Patrick Moore and David Hardy**
**Mitchell Beazley, 1972**

**The Discovery of the Universe**
**by Tony Osman**
**Usborne, 1975**

**The Story of Astronomy**
**by Patrick Moore**
**Macdonald & Co., 1972**

**The Universe**
**by Robin Kerrod**
**Sampson Low, 1975**

**The Young Scientist Book of**
**Spaceflight**
**by Kenneth Gatland**
**Usborne, 1976**